A PRIVATE MATTER

by

RONALD MAVOR

for Ken [...]

Ronald Mavor

5 Gloucester Place
Edinburgh.

S A M U E L F R E N C H

LONDON

NEW YORK TORONTO SYDNEY HOLLYWOOD

Printed in Great Britain by
Biddles Ltd, Guildford, Surrey.

Photograph by courtesy of George A. Oliver, D.A.

This play was first performed under the title "A Life of the General" at the Nottingham Playhouse on 26th January, 1972. The cast was as follows:

ANTHONY   Derek Fowlds
CHRISTOPHER   Donald Douglas
ANNE   Dorothy Reynolds
MERVYN   Robin Bailey

Directed by David William; designed by Robin Pidcock.

The play was first produced in London by H. M. Tennent Ltd. and Knightsbridge Theatrical Productions Ltd., at the Vaudeville Theatre on 21st February, 1973. The cast was as follows:

ANTHONY   Derek Fowlds
CHRISTOPHER   Peter Cellier
ANNE   Dorothy Reynolds
MERVYN   Alastair Sim

Directed by Ian McKellen; designed by Hutchinson Scott.

A PRIVATE MATTER

ACT ONE

The Drawing Room of Lady Black-Matheson's country house in the South of England.

It is small but correct: Adam fireplace, wall brackets, a landscape over the mantelpiece, chintzy curtains, an off-white sofa and two armchairs, mahogany tables with The Field, *what you would expect . . . It was probably done up twenty years ago by Harrods.*

It is seven o'clock of an autumn evening. The time is the present.

Christopher (41) has been sorting a pile of cards at a small desk and is putting them into a large brief-case. He wears a dinner jacket. Anthony (26) is lying on the sofa reading a magazine, "Nova" probably. He wears a cravat and broad-collared shirt with a sharp, but respectable, suit and leather slippers.

There is a knock on the door from Anne's foot, to which at first no attention is paid, but finally Christopher, with some irritation, opens the door and Anne enters carrying a large tray with drinks. She is an elegant and quite formidable lady of sixty-plus and is "dressed for dinner"

Anne	Thank you, Kit. At least you opened the door. I wish to goodness one or other of you would be a bit of help. Neither of you lifts a hand to help me and you know I'm in a state. I've never met such a pair of stupid, unhelpful ruffians as you two and it would serve you right if I were to die and leave you to stew in your own juice. I might as well save my breath. You'd starve, the pair of you. You're so jolly idle and useless you'd starve if you were shipwrecked in the middle of Fortnum and Mason's. Anthony, honey, go and get dressed.
Anthony	I am dressed.
Anne	Is he not going to put on a dinner jacket?
Christopher	You'd better ask him.

Anne   Are you not going to put on a dinner jacket?
                Anthony shakes his head

                Please, honey. I told Mr. Dakyns we would dress for
                dinner, because I want him to get a good impression.
                He'll get a horrible impression if he sees you lying
                about like . . . a Pop group or something. Sweetheart,
                I like pretty clothes, too, but they're not suitable.
                Anthony, please go and change.

Anthony   I have changed.

Anne   I can't, I can't understand you. Have you no feeling
                for me? Do you not *want* to help me? Haven't I
                enough to do? I've spent three days slaving in the
                kitchen for this dinner and Mrs. Robertson has been
                scrubbing like a fiend.

Christopher   It won't make any difference to him. He'll never
                notice it.

Anne   It'll make a difference to me. It's very important that
                we all make a good impression. Obviously we won't be
                on his intellectual level but at least we can make things
                nice.

Anthony   *I'm* on his intellectual level.

Anne   Well, I'm not. I'm not ashamed to admit it. I'm going
                to make an absolute fool of myself. He'll ask me
                questions and I won't be able to remember a thing. I
                can't think what sort of impression we're going to
                make. So you're both to help me, do you understand?

Anthony   We'll look after him.

Anne   That's what I'm afraid of. He wants to know what
                your father was like and all I can show him is you
                two. I really don't know what sort of book he's
                going to write. It'll be a horror comic if you pair have
                anything to do with it. And please tidy up that desk.

Christopher   Don't get so excited. Calm down.

Anne   How can I not get excited? You're both so
                insensitive.

Anthony   Don't use foul language.

Anne   I don't know what to do with you. Kit, help me.

Christopher   Help you with what?

Anne   Your brother for one thing.

Anthony	Thank you.
Christopher	You want him to change?
Anne	At least I want him to wash.
Anthony	I have washed.
Christopher	*(after a brief inspection)* Yes, he has.
Anne	He could comb his hair .
Christopher	He likes it like that.
Anne	He could at least sit up.
Christopher	Go on. Sit up.
	Anthony does so
Anthony	Marvellous discipline. Like the army.
Anne	And stop sneering at the army.
Anthony	Who's for a drink?
Christopher	Gin and pink.
Anne	We must wait for Mr. Dakyns. It's impolite to start.
Anthony	Mother. Relax. Mr. Dakyns is an intelligent man. He s a don. Don's are intelligent. That means they don't jump to conclusions. Relax.
Anne	First impressions are very important.
Anthony	He's had his first impressions. He's had a nice genteel tea. I've come all the way down from London and taken him for a brisk walk to the windmill. You've been very gracious. Kit's been out of the way with his Tory ladies. He's had a bath. The water was hot; for once. Now he's squeezing into his 1930 dinner jacket and his patent leather shoes ready to make the most devastating impression on *us.*
Anne	I hope the çreme brulée is alright.
Anthony	If it's not, it'll be tremendous fun. It'll make us all madly chummy. We'll laugh about it for days. It'll make a jolly footnote in his book.
Anne	Did you remember the brandy?
Christopher	Yes. It's in the boot of the car.
Anne	It's not much use to us there, is it?
Christopher	I'll get it.
Anne	You do nothing to help.
Christopher	Don't nag.

Anthony	Well, I'm going to have a drink. I can't make a good impression unless I have a couple of good gins, Ma?
Anne	No, thank you. I'll wait until our guest comes.
Anthony	Big brother?
Christopher	Pink gin, and not too much water.
Anne	I'm going to the kitchen. But, honestly you're to mind your manners. I mean that.

She goes out. A pause

Christopher	How did you find him?
Anthony	You should have come yourself.
Christopher	I had to look in to the office.
Anthony	Why?
Christopher	I hadn't managed to get in in the morning . . .
Anthony	And all your adoring Tory ladies can't get through the day without a smile from the boss.
Christopher	I have to go through the mail.
Anthony	Jesus.
Christopher	Don't sneer at me. Just what do you do in *your* office? It's quite a difficult period in the constituency. We can't weaken now.
Anthony	Firm hand on the tiller.
Christopher	*(exercising considerable self-control)* How did you find this Dakyns chap?
Anthony	He's quite bright. A good deal of elegant chat but I'd think he's quite a smart cookie underneath.
Christopher	I'm not sure I like the idea of a smart cookie writing about father. Why is he so determined to write a book about him?
Anthony	He didn't say. He makes jokes.
Christopher	*(quickly)* What kind of jokes?
Anthony	He says that after a cardinal and a politician he thought he'd like to do a General.
Christopher	Oh, that kind of joke. I find it a little tasteless, I must say.
Anthony	I thought it was quite funny. I hope he goes on being tasteless.

Christopher	Mr. Dakyns presented himself to us as a scholar. And he was in the army. I expect him to behave honourably and in the manner of a gentleman.
Anthony	You're a *dinosaur.*
Christopher	I do have an old-fashioned regard for decent behaviour, if that's what you mean. I'm not going to let this chap write about father if he's going to be anything but honourable and serious. I'm quite clear about that. Father suffered enough when he was alive without having . . . I don't know . . . smart intellectuals writing about him when he's dead. I'm not at all sure mother was right to have him down.
Anthony	She said you were all for it.
Christopher	Yes, she did. I am. Yes, we decided we should see the chap and . . . Yes, I decided it would be a good idea . . . if he makes a decent job of it. There ought to be a book about the Old Man.
Anthony	Why?
Christopher	Don't be silly.
Anthony	Tell me why.
Christopher	Because he was a distinguished soldier and one of the youngest Generals in the War.
Anthony	Super.
Christopher	I know it doesn't mean anything to you, but I was jolly proud of father at that time. At school everybody knew about him and . . . I suppose you think we should just have let Hitler win the War?
Anthony	Relax.
Christopher	You just don't think at all, you people. You want to knock everything down. But what would you put in it's place? I wish you'd tell me that.
Anthony	I'm going to need some more gin.
	He goes to help himself. As he does so Mervyn Dakyns comes in. He is a big man who looks like, and is, a don who has been around.
	Probably rimless glasses and a rather elegant dinner jacket, neither too High Table nor too Late Night Line-Up
Anthony	Ah. Come in. What will you drink?

Mervyn	I'll take some of your excellent Black Label.
Anthony	Ice?
Mervyn	Do you have ice? Yes, please, one cube. I deplore the American habit of giving you a miniature Himalayan ice-field with a little drop of whisky at the bottom.
Anthony	You get a cold nose.
Mervyn	It's supposed to be a healthy sign at Crufts.
Christopher	Enjoy your walk?
Mervyn	Yes, very much. We didn't go very far, but I like to get the lie of the land.
Anthony	In case you have to make a quick getaway,
Mervyn	No. I hadn't anticipated that. Cheers. You're quite happy about my writing this book about your father?
Christopher	Yes. I think so.
Mervyn	I've really become terribly interested in him.
Anthony	We were wondering why.
Mervyn	Why I should want to write a Life of General Black-Matheson? All the other Generals have had books. Most of them have written them themselves — which is bully for them because they can tell terrible lies — and your father seemed to me — You know that I served with him, however briefly, when I was a very junior Staff Officer. He seemed to me a remarkable example of the man of action. And I wanted to do a man of action. They speak louder than words, as someone or other said. Also I must confess that your father's tragedy . . . I think it was a tragedy. Was it a tragedy? Anyway, the ending of his career . . . was something quite, quite unexpected and . . . Will your mother talk about it, do you think?
Anthony	She never has.
Mervyn	Really?
Christopher	It's not a thing we talk about very much.
Mervyn	I do hope she'll talk to me. She is a most charming person. Why won't she talk about it?
Christopher	I really couldn't say.
Mervyn	I'm sorry. You mustn't allow me to probe.
Christopher	It's quite all right.

Mervyn	You'll find I do probe sometimes. It's only because I am so interested. You mustn't let me be rude, whatever you do. I do hope you'll both understand and be on my side. I have a very high regard for your father. I want to do him justice. He deserves a good book. Don't you think so?
Christopher	*(a pause)* Yes. Of course.
Anthony	Do people *deserve* a good book?
Mervyn	Why not? You deserve a good reputation, a nice house, a good job, even a good hammering sometimes. I think it's an appropriate phrase. But all I meant was that, after everything that happened, and in all the circumstances. I would like to put a fair and full account on the record. Do you not agree?
Christopher	Of course.
Anthony	I'm all for it.
Mervyn	But when I say fair and full, I mean fair and full. Can we just establish that, right at the beginning?
Christopher	I'm not sure I know what you mean?
Mervyn	Oh? I wonder if Anthony does?
Anthony	Dramatic revelations in the 'Sunday Times'.
Mervyn	Oh, no. I wouldn't want to do that and I'm sure there's nothing I could sell to the 'News of the World'. Certainly not.
Christopher	I don't think this is a matter you should joke about, Mr. Dakyns.
Mervyn	I agree with you. Sorry. I'm inclined to joke about. But may I take it a little further? Beneath my jovial exterior I am always very deeply serious. You may have got the impression that I write these books as a kind of hobby. In a sense I do. But as well as being a deeply respected member of one of our oldest and most respected provincial universities — Cambridge — I have acquired a modest reputation as a biographer. I regard this as being quite as much a professional commitment on my part as teaching idle youths the study of History. So if I go ahead with the book it is on the basis that I write as fair an account of your father's life and as full a study of his ideas and motivations as I'm capable of — warts and all. I've

stated my admiration for him but I guess we'll come
upon one or two delicate matters — won't we — as we
go along. I shall use the velvet glove, of course, the
surgeon's rubber glove rather than the mailed fist of
sensational journalism. But I am going to have to
open up the patient. I am the dentist saying, "Perhaps
this is going to hurt". I hope very much that it will
hurt very little. But sometimes in the treatment of
one's patient, if I may extend the metaphor, one has
to pluck out a rooted tooth, an inflamed sorrow. I
don't suppose you've read either of my books?

Christopher   I've sent for them.

Mervyn   Ah. I think you'll see what I mean. Biography
               nowadays is quite different from hagiography. I feel
               it's more honest. We get nearer the truth. And I believe
               the Bible when it says that if you know the truth, the
               truth will make you whole — even if I don't believe a
               great deal else it says. Have I alarmed you? I do want
               you all on my side and I felt I should explain my
               position. I'm rather an honest man, in my fashion.

Christopher   I think you know that my mother . . . that we've all
               lived under a strong sense of grievance about how my
               father was treated. We feel he never got his due. *(a
               pause)* I want you to write the book.

Mervyn   And Anthony?

Anthony   Anthony's bloody determined you write the book.

Mervyn   So that's all right, then.

Christopher   At least, once we've got to know you. Once we've
               decided that we can trust you, that you're the right
               person for the job.

Mervyn   You can trust me.

Christopher   I didn't mean to imply . . .

Mervyn   My life is an open book. Two open books, and twenty-
               five years of honest, unremitting, academic toil. My
               credentials are immaculate. And my books even sell.
               You couldn't put yourself in better hands.

Christopher   I checked up.

Anthony   Mother used to go to dances with your Vice-
               Chancellor.

Mervyn	What better recommendation could I have than that? I used to go to dances with the wife . . . with one who is now the wife of a Bishop. So I have access to the lowdown on half the curates in England. You'd be astonished how useful it has been in all sorts of ways.
Christopher	We want you to write the book.
Mervyn	Oh, good. Thank you. You said you had a strong sense of, was it grievance? Can we talk about that for a minute? Why?
Christopher	I would have thought it was pretty obvious.
Mervyn	You think your father was unjustly treated?
Christopher	Of course. Everyone thought so. Everyone who knew anything about it. Or at least harshly treated. No, it was unjust. I really prefer not to talk about it.
Anthony	*(to Mervyn)* Go on.
Mervyn	Perhaps this isn't the time. I'm sorry.
Anthony	No. Go on. If you're going to write a Life of General Black-Matheson we can't all behave like a bloody Trappist monastery.
Christopher	And you shut up.
Mervyn	It's my fault. One shouldn't ask difficult questions before dinner. I can very well understand that even after -- what is it — twenty-eight years . . . something like this still casts a shadow. Your father died, when, about ten years ago? He hadn't forgotten it?
Christopher	He never spoke about it.
Mervyn	I shall just have to charm Lady Black-Matheson into confiding in me.
Christopher	I don't think you should ask her about . . . why he came back from France and all that kind of thing.
Mervyn	No?
Christopher	As I said, we never talk about it and I'm not sure it would be a good idea to start doing so now.
Mervyn	I don't think I can accept that. It would be a major inhibition.
Christopher	It's not as if we've anything to hide. It's just that it upsets my mother and nobody really knows what happened, so it would be a pity to start digging up a lot of disagreeable . . . We don't know what happened.

Mervyn	You don't know what happened?
Christopher	Well. There were various stories . . .
Mervyn	I know what happened.
Christopher	What? How do you know?
Mervyn	I was with the Staff at the time and, as it happened, the confidential report came across my desk.
Christopher	This puts a completely different complexion on the whole business. I'm astounded. If I'd known that you knew about the . . . and particularly if I'd known that you intended making use of a confidential military document, we certainly wouldn't have invited you down to the house.
Anthony	Kit, you're making yourself look even more pompous and silly than usual.
Christopher	Let me handle this.
Anthony	Handle what? Mr. Dakyns proposes to write a biography of father. Father's life has only three interesting episodes: two good battles and a successfully hushed-up scandal. I doubt if even the three put together make anything a sane man would pay five guineas for; but if you're going to forbid the chap even to mention one of them, he might as well pack it in and go home.
Christopher	That's not the point. It's a matter of principle.
Anthony	What principle?
Christopher	If you haven't the nous to understand, keep your mouth shut.
Mervyn	Perhaps I may assure you, Christopher, that I have no intention whatever of using any document; nor do I possess the document. It is true, however, that fortuitously I came to know, and do know, what happened.
Christopher	Well, in that case . . .
Mervyn	But you can trust me, and I hope you will. I was in the army. I was a fellow officer of your father's. I knew that only a few of the officers, even in the regiment, were aware of what had happened. The whole matter was treated at the time not only as one of some delicacy, but as a Top Secret.
Christopher	I can trust you to say nothing about it?

Mervyn	You mustn't put words in my mouth.
Christopher	What do you mean by that?
Mervyn	That I have the highest regard for your father's reputation, and that you can trust me not willingly to harm it.
Christopher	Well, I tell you frankly I don't like it.
Mervyn	I'm sorry if it was a shock to you. But there, the worst is over now. When you have time to read my books you will be reassured, I'm certain.

Enter Anne

Anne	I'm so sorry to have deserted you, but I have no staff, not even a cook. So I have to rush off to the kitchen and turn knobs every ten minutes or so. Are the boys keeping you entertained? Or are you entertaining them? Have they given you a drink? Your glass is empty. Anthony, give Mr. Dakyns a drink. What was it you were having?
Mervyn	Whisky. Thank you.
Anne	I'm going to sit down. I think I would like a little gin. Well, now. It is nice to have an intelligent visitor. We seem to see nobody down here but the locals and friends of Christopher's and Anthony's.
Anthony	So we don't have any intelligent visitors.
Anne	They trip me up, everything I say. What have you been talking about?
Mervyn	Shop, I'm afraid, a little.
Anne	You've been talking about your book? And I've missed it. What have you said? Do you have some kind of shape for it already in your mind? It must be very interesting. But it's rude to ask you questions. We mustn't talk about it until after dinner.
Mervyn	I would like to talk about it, Lady Black-Matheson. At the moment it's really my only subject — apart from French politics in the latter half of the seventeenth century; which is not a subject most people can be particularly scintillating about. But perhaps you can? One mustn't jump to conclusions.
Anne	I don't think I can even be scintillating about my husband.

| Mervyn | I would like to talk about him. This *is* a working visit, isn't it? I wouldn't have thrust myself on your hospitality otherwise. |

| Anne | We're delighted to have you. I see so few people from the old days, you know, who served with my husband. It's one of the perils of living in the country. One loses touch. You're going to find me very silly; but I must try to collect my thoughts. Now what would you like me to tell you? |

| Mervyn | No, no, no. This is going too far in the other direction. I'm not going to conduct an inquisition. Not while your mind is still on the cooking. It might ruin our dinner. What I would like . . . what I hope is that we can just talk. You know? I'd like you to think of me as someone, "from the old days" if you like, who knew your husband a little, served with him, and would like to know more about him, twenty-five years later. I'd hate you to think of me as a man with a little black book and a pencil. I never take notes. Fortunately I have a splendid memory. I can remember anything for a week though nothing for much longer than that. But I have a dictating machine in College and a buxom lady typist, so I manage. |

A pause

Anne	That must be very nice.
Anthony	What must? The lady typist?
Mervyn	I take it as a good sign that Anthony has already begun pulling my leg. It makes me feel at home. I find that we have two kinds of students nowadays; those that start off being witty, cynical and supercilious about their teachers, and those that only get like that after a couple of terms. On the whole I prefer the former. You can mark them down as enemies from the beginning.
Anthony	Then you know where you are.
Mervyn	Precisely.
Anne	You make the University sound a terrible place.
Mervyn	My dear lady, don't you read the newspapers? We go in fear of our lives.
Anne	How dreadful. Why do you stay?

Mervyn	So few of us have any useful talents. The more foresighted of us write books, cadge invitations to appear on television, and try to pass ourselves off as literati in the hope of escaping the paving stones and the petrol bombs. In fact, it's not the bombs that are alarming; it's the thought of having hundreds of unwashed revolutionaries squatting in one's rooms; keeping their guitars in one's bath.
Anne	Kit, I do wish you'd go and bring in the brandy. I have asked you before.
Christopher	I'll look after it.
Anne	For some reason these boys expect to be waited on hand and foot. You'd think we still had the army. Soldiers make perfect servants. They're so polite and peaceful.
Anthony	Join the Army; it's so polite and peaceful.
Mervyn	Is there anything I can do? I mean, to help in the kitchen.
Anne	Goodness, no. But, thank you. Everything's more or less under control.
Mervyn	You must find these very changed days, after the army and . . .
Anne	Well, yes. But of course everyone had servants when our generation was young. It wasn't just the army. But our whole life was a series of changes. A soldier's life is never the same for very long. He has to . . .
Anthony	*(sotto voce)* follow the drum.
Anne	. . . go where he's sent. We were lucky, on the whole. I was able to go with John almost everywhere. Of course it meant that we never had a proper home when we were young, but . . . when you're young it doesn't seem to matter. And now we have this rather *nice* home, I'm not sure it's much better.
Mervyn	"Better a dinner of herbs where love is than a stalled ox and hatred therewith". I'm sorry. That's not a very suitable quotation. I mean that, when your husband was alive . . .
Anne	That's exactly it. You couldn't have put it better. The boys hardly know I'm there, and . . . Anthony, give me a little more gin. It's true, Mr. Dakyns, but it doesn't make for very lively conversation before

dinner. I do wish you'd known my husband really
well. He was a fine man. He was always kind and
considerate . . . not only to me. I miss him terribly.

Mervyn   I'm sure you do.

Anne   He seemed to be naturally sympathetic to people.
It's fashionable nowadays to pretend that the army is
very rough, that they're a bullying, bunch of thugs or
something, but it isn't at all. You know that. I've met
so many cultivated, gentle, kind officers. A nice
young man looks so much nicer in scarlet and a
smart haircut. They were so polite. I do think there's
something to be said for manners, don't you? For
some kind of formality.

Mervyn   Of course.

Anne   These boys couldn't care less. Christopher has
manners but manages to be rude at the same time
and Anthony just does what he likes. He'd be happier
in a pig-sty.

Christopher   Mother.

Anne   What?

Christopher   I'm not sure Mr. Dakyns is interested in our family
squabbles.

Anthony   (bringing her a drink) Are you sure you should have
this?

Anne   Aren't they tiresome, Mr. Dakyns? They treat me
like a dotty aunt. Thank you, dear. When he was
young my husband used to be terribly keen on
shooting. When we were in Italy we would go away
on our own to a little shooting hut in the mountains.
Some mornings I would wake up and find him gone.
And he would tramp miles over the hills and come
back in the darkness with a bag full of little dead
animals and I had to help him to skin and pluck them
and make some kind of pie. He loved a game pie. I
wasn't good at that sort of thing but of course I had
to pretend that I enjoyed it. It's funny; looking back
now these seem very happy times — in the mountains.
And then at a certain point he just said to me "I
don't like killing animals". He didn't explain why or
anything. He just stopped. After that he gave away
his trophies. We had quite a display of horns and
antlers mounted on wooden shields. He gave them to

his club. We had to hire a small van. I think that was the happiest night of my life — to see them going away. It was such a silly thing, but I was always jealous of the animals.

A pause

Christopher	Father was a jolly good shot.
Mervyn	Was he? *(to Anne)* Why do you think he stopped?
Anne	Stopped shooting? I've no idea. He just seemed to get tired of it.
Mervyn	Doesn't it seem a little surprising?
Anthony	It seems to me a very sensible thing to do.
Christopher	I was always told he was a jolly good shot. Can't see why he should give it up.
Mervyn	*(to Anne)* I'm sorry. Do go on.
Anne	He used to paint, too, you know. When he was young he was very interested in painting but it wasn't thought a suitable occupation. But he did water-colours. That's one of his . . . when we were in Italy.
Mervyn	I was admiring it.
Anne	I tried to get him to paint more, to take up oils after the War. I thought it might have been good for him; but he wouldn't give up his old box of water-colours. He could have been a great painter I'm sure.
Anthony	Actually he was a terrible painter. He painted like a Victorian governess. I saw him once with this little box of paints and a block and he was terribly fussy about changing the water and keeping his brushes clean. He niggled away with little bits of rag torn from old shirts and the final result was awful.
Christopher	I like his pictures.
Anthony	That's the final condemnation. They're the kind of pictures Kit likes.
Christopher	Very funny.
Anne	I don't see why you should mock them.
Anthony	I'm not mocking them. They're very bad pictures. Finish.
Anne	You can't accept that anyone older than you can know anything about art. You resent our generation, though you don't mind coming down here and eating my food.

Anthony	Don't write an opera about it. I'm an ignorant bastard but I know a little about art. I admit it's commercial art but that simply means one has to have a little professional competence. You will load everything with emotional value judgements. I loved father dearly but he was a rotten painter. So what?
Anne	We don't all have time to hang around the smart London galleries like you, of course, so we're bound to be stupid and ill-informed.
Anthony	I didn't say that. I don't even believe it.
Anne	I don't think we have to fight about it. You have the time and the interest, to keep up with all this modern art and I'm happy that you should have. You're very knowledgeable about art.
Anthony	It's more that I make a living at it — if you call the kind of design work we do art.
Anne	You are knowledgeable. You were always interested in art.
Anthony	Isn't it nice?
Anne	And what does that mean?
Anthony	It means that whether or not I'm knowledgeable, as you say, about art, I resent your making capital out of it. "Anthony's very knowledgeable about art". You don't know what it means, but you think it gives you a certain kudos. "Anthony plays the piano — really very well", you told that fading Madame Recamier the other day. He doesn't. He plays it bloody awfully. The average ten year old schoolgirl plays it better. But she doesn't have the privilege of being your son, so she doesn't count.
Anne	I don't understand you.
Anthony	Well, leave me alone.
Anne	What am I to do? I can't even talk in a civil manner to my children.
Mervyn	I used to play the piano. I won a prize once for arpeggios. It was a little plaster bust of Beethoven. What a world it conjures up. I'm sure nowadays they don't teach arpeggios. Or do they? You find the piano difficult?
Anthony	It's very difficult.

Mervyn	And art? Even commercial art?
Anthony	It's very difficult too. Perhaps I've worked harder at it.
Mervyn	Or perhaps it's your real vocation.
Anthony	Jesus. My real vocation is lying in the sun, and sleeping. And sex.
Christopher	Your vocation is being an idle sod.
Anthony	That's what I said.
Anne	You must find this a charming conversation, Mr. Dakyns.
Mervyn	I'm finding it very interesting. And not lacking in charm.
Anthony	I'm doing my best.
Christopher	It's a thoroughly imbecile conversation.
Anthony	But interesting.
Christopher	I don't find it interesting.
Anthony	You don't have the biographer's interest in this strange Black-Matheson family that Mr. Dakyns has.
Mervyn	I didn't say that.
Anthony	But we are kind of zoo animals, to you, aren't we?
Anne	That's a nasty remark.
Mervyn	And it's not true. I do wish you wouldn't call me Mr. Dakyns. Mervyn isn't much of a name but if you would be so kind as to call me Mervyn it might be better. You can't accuse someone called Mervyn of peering at you down a microscope. Would you allow me to call you Anne?
Anne	Of course.
Mervyn	I don't want to peer at you.
Anne	Of course you don't. You're both being intolerable. It's when the two of you get together that you're so unpleasant. Christopher, go down to the garage — bring up the brandy. We can go through quite soon but I like to know that everything's in order.
Christopher	Did you wash Aunt Lucy's glasses?
Anne	Yes.

Exit Christopher

Anne	I have to ask them twenty times to do the simplest little things. Now Mervyn, tell me something about Oxford.
Mervyn	Cambridge.
Anne	I'm sorry.
Mervyn	I was rather sorry myself. I feel I'm more of an Oxford person. I have a slight air of dampness and a donnish wit. I try to master it, of course, but I've never aspired to be what you might call "Cambridge". I could never live up to King's College Chapel — that ceiling and all that polyphony. Of course Cambridge is full of scientists nowadays — scientists and oarsmen — and evangelists for Voluntary Service Overseas. We're all trying desperately to catch up with Oxfam.
Anne	But it must be lovely to live there.
Mervyn	It's agreeable.
Anne	I'm sure you love it; in spite of what you say about the students.
Mervyn	It's nice during the vacations — except that you have to get used to being photographed by American tourists. It's a little like a zoo. They try to make us feel at home and forget about the jungle, but one is limited. It was when I went back after the War and they stroked and patted me and offered me this nice warm cage, that I'm afraid I just settled down. They keep my fur sleek and glistening and see that I get enough exercise and the right kind of food; so they know I won't run away. Anthony will quite correctly regard me as a fossil. I am, but I have managed to retain the faintest fraction of self-criticism — just enough to tell me, once in a blue moon, in the long watches of the night that I am an anchorite chained in my cell and rapidly losing the use of my limbs. A year or two and I shan't be able to walk.
	That's really why I've taken to writing books. They may be donnish books but they do sell outside the University. They're the messages in bottles I throw into the sea, to let somebody know I'm still alive. And that's why I want terribly to write this book about your husband.

Anne	I don't quite understand.
Mervyn	It was a seed planted in the mind — an eagle feather I picked up on the moor. I could never decide to do a book — I mean apart from the kind of book that you make out of your lecture notes and sell to your students as a form of revenge — I would never do this kind of book for that kind of reason. You realise that some incident, some meeting, something seen or heard, has stayed fresh in the memory. It must have been working or it would have got rusty like an old railway track. There's been something going backwards and forwards along that line even if I haven't noticed it. You never know what it is until you take time off to explore. You watch through long moonless nights — and one night you hear a train. You follow it over unknown country — and perhaps you find a smugglers' cave. It's full of gold doubloons and pieces of eight.
Anne	And you feel that my husband's life is going to be one of your railways?
Mervyn	I had a brief meeting with your husband, which has stayed in my mind, but working away. And now I have the privilege of meeting his family; and, I hope, of being allowed to talk about him. I regard that as a treasure.
Anthony	Come now.
Mervyn	I do.
Anthony	But that's not what you were talking about.
Mervyn	Yes. Yes it was.
Anthony	But what else? Why has it grabbed you the way it has?
Mervyn	That's one of life's mysteries.
Anthony	Aw, come on. You were saying that you have a deep emotional reason for wanting to write this book.
Anne	Anthony.
Mervyn	Was I? I can't think of any reason.
Anthony	You've suppressed it.
Mervyn	I do hate that psychiatrist's jargon.
Anthony	What's the reason?
Mervyn	If I've suppressed it, I won't know, will I?

Anthony	Abreact, man. Abreact. It'll come.
Mervyn	You don't even understand your own terminology.
Anne	Anthony. Stop it. I don't know what you're talking about, but I know you're not being civil to Mr. Dakyns. Now I insist on your being well behaved in my house — at least when we have a guest.
Mervyn	I don't think Anthony's being rude. Believe me, young people talk like this all the time.
Anne	He's being what I call rude; but perhaps I'm old-fashioned.
Mervyn	I don't think he means to be.
Anthony	No, I don't mean to be. I just want to know about Mervyn's motivation. It fascinates me.
Anne	I won't have Mr. Dakyns, Mervyn, bullied.
Anthony	He likes it. It excites him. A red rag to a bull.
Mervyn	All right. We must talk about it sometime. But I hardly feel this is the moment to bare our souls. do you?
Anthony	Aw, come on. Spill the beans.
Anne	Gracious. I must go and turn off the oven. Anthony. Please be nice. Will you give me two minutes, and then come through? I have to dish the soup and do one or two other things. It'll be a very simple little dinner, I'm afraid, as I have to do everything myself.
Mervyn	You're sure I can't help?
Anne	Perfectly sure. If you'll excuse me, I need a minute's peace and everything'll be all right. Anthony'll give you another drink if you want one. I'm sorry we're being so awful. Just two minutes.

Exit Anne. Mervyn opens the door for her

Anne	Thank you.
Anthony	Well. What about it?
Mervyn	What about what?
Anthony	The motivation; why you want to write this book?
Mervyn	At the moment I'm not very sure that I do.
Anthony	Come now.

Mervyn	I don't think I want to be sniped at. It seems to me that you and your brother are both against me — and from opposite sides. I'm caught in a positive enfilading fire. Christopher thinks I'm going to let his side down by publishing a regimental secret and you, if I'm not mistaken think I'm going to indulge a secret passion for . . . what?
Anthony	You tell me.
Mervyn	I'm too old a hand to want to play confessions with you.
Anthony	It can be fun.
Mervyn	Only at a certain age. You've got me wrong.
Anthony	Why should your meeting with the old man make such an impression?
Mervyn	I don't know. He was quite an impressive chap.
Anthony	Did he say anything memorable?
Mervyn	Not that I remember.
Anthony	Are you interested in tactics?
Mervyn	He fought two very brilliant battles.
Anthony	So they say, but you'd hardly get hooked on that.
Mervyn	He was a remarkable leader.
Anthony	They were ten a penny.
Mervyn	I don't think they were. They never are.
Anthony	So it must have been the crash. The downfall of the General.
Mervyn	It probably was.
Anthony	You know exactly what happened?
Mervyn	Yes.
Anthony	You saw a Report?
Mervyn	I did.
Anthony	How full a Report?
Mervyn	You know the story, of course?
Anthony	I know the story; but not of course.
Mervyn	Why not? You don't talk about it? You've never talked about it?
Anthony	Never.
Mervyn	How strange.
Anthony	Strange? It's downright demented.

Mervyn	But you found out? How? You must have been . . . You were hardly born when it happened.
Anthony	I was nearly aborted by it.
Mervyn	How did you find out? Christopher would tell you.
Anthony	Christopher wouldn't tell the Recording Angel. Mother told me it was a conspiracy. I think she believes that herself. Or she's convinced herself that's what it was. Kit's made rather a fetish of turning pale and being tight-lipped whenever the subject's mentioned — as you saw. I guess he found out when he was in the Regiment. I rather suspect that that was why he left it.
Mervyn	So you found out on your own?
Anthony	About seven or eight years ago, not long after father died, we got a Christmas card from the old R.S.M. saying he'd retired and was living in a cottage in Surrey, just outside Woking. I knew he'd been there because he made some sort of oblique reference to the incident. So I went down to see him. I was petrified, but I was bloody determined to find out the whole ghastly truth once and for all. He told me. And do you know, I laughed all the way back in the train to Waterloo. I was hysterical. Everyone thought I was stoned. I still think it's bloody funny.
Mervyn	It wasn't funny at the time. And it must have been anything but funny for your father . . . and your mother.
Anthony	R.S.M. Macdonald was there and thought it was kind of bloody funny.
Mervyn	I can't altogether agree.
Anthony	The regiment were hanging about back in Normandy, regrouping or something — the regiment the Old Man used to belong to. He'd been up at advance headquarters having a very rough time with the battle of Caen and the Falaise gap and all that, so when things began to get better they sent him back for a few days with his old chums as a kind of rest cure.
Mervyn	It was just after Paris was liberated and we all started dashing off in the general direction of Berlin.

Anthony   Of course they're delighted to see him, and the
            Colonel says something like, "I say, old boy, d'you
            realise that next Sunday's the tenth of September".
            or whatever it was, when they had this Founder's
            Day Parade. So they're sufficiently far from the
            fighting and sufficiently idle to put the whole thing
            on in his honour. Fantastic, in the middle of a war.
            Everybody out there on the square, military band
            and all. Atten . . shun. General salute. Present arms.
            The old man has been sitting in his room struggling
            into a stiff collar and stiffer boots — I've seen them
            — and a fancy dress uniform that they flew over
            specially from London, with scrambled egg round his
            hat and bits of torn ribbon plastered across his chest,
            and no doubt helping himself to about a bottle of
            whisky to dull the acute sense of meaninglessness of
            the whole damned nonsense. What does he do? He
            takes the lot off, flings it on the bed and patters
            down the stairs absolutely starkers. So what?
            Nobody's got hurt. Old Macdonald hustles him into
            the ante-room and whistles for the Colonel. They
            carry on with the parade without him, rustle him
            upstairs in a blanket while the band plays the Eton
            Boating Song outside, and that's it. They have a
            council of war, shoot him off home, relieve him of
            his command, make him G.O.C. Training, or
            something, which means he goes out to Aldershot
            once a week and says, "Jolly good show. Carry on,
            chaps", and somebody else takes his command and
            probably gets himself shot crossing the Rhine. I
            think it's a bloody funny story; a bloody funny
            story.

Mervyn   It's not really.

Anthony   They get half a dozen army psychiatrists up in
            Scotland to look at him and invent some sort of
            suitable diagnosis. Everybody's hellish solemn.
            "Jolly bad luck". "Poor old Black Jack". "Had a
            hard war". If you're going to write this book you've
            to tell the truth, Mervyn, and the truth is that the
            old man was as sane as the rest of them, standing
            about with feathers in their hats on a summer
            morning in the middle of a war. Now, will you say
            that?

Mervyn	I don't think I can say that exactly.
Anthony	Why not?
Mervyn	It *was* rather an eccentric gesture; and it ruined your father's career.
Anthony	All right. So it did. But what kind of career was it anyway?
Mervyn	It was a distinguished and honourable career.
Anthony	Killing people.
Mervyn	*(shrugs)*
Anthony	Isn't that what old soldiers do?
Mervyn	You don't really take as simple a view as that, do you?
Anthony	Maybe it prevented his getting himself killed.
Mervyn	So you think it was a good thing?
Anthony	I just don't think it's particularly tragic to stay alive.
Mervyn	That's what you want me to say in the book?
Anthony	I want you to say that the people who pretended that it was a tragedy were wrong. That the people who pretended it was a terrible disgrace were crazy — notably us. What you've to do, Mervyn, is blast open this family cupboard and say, "Look, friends, it's just a few old, dry bones". That's what *I* want you to do.
Mervyn	That isn't quite what I had in mind.
Anthony	Look. Bugger the book. I came back from that journey to Woking a changed man. I trailed down there a guilt-ridden, spotty, adolescent and I was liberated.
Mervyn	The road to Damascus.
Anthony	But could I tell them? You don't know what this family's like. Beneath our smooth middle class exteriors we're positively Charles Addams. I'd rather they kept the old man's ashes in a bowl on the mantelpiece and stirred them with a crucifix whenever there was a full moon. But they just won't talk about him at all. The shame. The unmentionable disgrace of letting the side down. It wouldn't have mattered if he had robbed a bank or murdered a couple of princes in the tower . . .
	Christopher enters. He is in a very bad temper

Christopher   I don't know why I'm expected to act as a sort of under-footman in this house. Dinner's ready. I wish you wouldn't park your car right in front of my garage door.

Anthony   Sorry. I moved it out of the rain. The roof leaks.

Christopher   Then you should buy a decent car. I don't like you leaving a wreck like that at the foot of our drive anyway. Mr. Dakyns, I've been thinking about this book of yours and I don't think we want a Life of my father. We needn't tell my mother just yet, but I can see it isn't going to work. We'll refund any expenses you may have had, so you won't be the poorer for it.

Mervyn   My dear fellow . . .

Christopher   I don't want mother upset and this whole business is still extremely painful to her. I wasn't in favour of her accepting your suggestion in the first place. It was a great mistake to invite you down.

Mervyn   I have no desire or intention to upset Lady Black-Matheson but equally I have not the slightest intention of allowing myself to be pushed around by you. Can we be quite clear about that? I am a completely free agent? I am nobody's hack. I write what I like without anybody's by-your-leave.

Christopher   You need the family's permission.

Mervyn   No I don't; although I would be glad of their co-operation.

Christopher   Well we can't give you it.

Anthony   Why not?

Christopher   You keep out of this.

Anthony   Kit, you're drunk.

Christopher   Watch it.

Anthony   Mervyn and I are getting on splendidly.

Mervyn   I do think you are being a little hasty. Can we avoid contention? You and I have had very little chance to talk, because you were . . . busy in the afternoon, Christopher. You may have misjudged me. I think so. I think, too, that you may have a false idea about the kind of book I'm going to write . . . that I hope you will agree to my writing. Can we not take a little longer to make up our minds?

Anthony	Pay no attention to Christopher.
Mervyn	No, I'm going to pay attention to Christopher.
Christopher	It isn't going to work.
Mervyn	I think I must be the judge of that.
Anthony	You stick at it, Mervyn. Don't let them put you off.
Mervyn	Did you say dinner was ready?
Christopher	Yes. I'm sorry if I was rude.
Mervyn	Not at all. I'm enjoying myself.

> *Exeunt*
> *End of Act One*

ACT TWO

SCENE ONE

The scene is the same. It is about an hour and a half later. The four are sitting drinking coffee and brandy. It is clear that Mervyn has been making most of the conversation and that Anne has been working fairly hard to keep up the impression of a spirited conversation. Christopher is brooding and Anthony is bored.

Anne
Why should parents find it so difficult to talk to their children nowadays? I was devoted to *my* father and could talk to him about everything. I could say anything to him. We had marvellous conversations. Christopher never has anything to say. Anthony can talk the hind leg off a donkey when he wants to but he simply uses my house as a boarding house. Well, you do. You never let me know when you're coming and I've even gone to call you for dinner and found that you've gone back to London.

> *A pause*

Mervyn
People don't talk as much as they used to. It's not only parents and children.

Anne
But it's so unsociable.

Mervyn
I don't think so. Young people are very affectionate to each other but they don't make speeches about it.

Anne
How can you get to know someone if you don't talk to him?

Mervyn	Nowadays you just say, "Hi" and that means you want to live together for the next five years. The elegant preliminaries to a relationship, which you and I had to indulge in, simply don't exist any longer. It may be a good thing. I would hesitate to make a judgement.
Anne	I don't understand young people. We simply never met people who behaved like . . . all those boys and girls today. And the parents don't seem to be able to do anything about it.
Anthony	*(standing up)* Do you mind if I take off my jacket?
Anne	Yes, I do.
Mervyn	It's such a pretty shirt.
Anne	Well, don't roll your sleeves up.
Anthony	*(who had begun to do so)* All right. I wasn't going to do a striptease.
Anne	There are certain proprieties which I like to observe. Come and sit down.
Anthony	Everybody gives orders in this house. It's like a barracks. I'm sorry. Good health.
Christopher	Perhaps we should have offered you port?
Mervyn	No thank you. I prefer brandy.
Christopher	A cigar?
Anthony	Yes.
Mervyn	Thank you.

> *Anthony has sprung up to get the cigars. He takes one and throws another to Christopher.*

Christopher	Don't you drink port at the High Table?
Mervyn	Quite. I find port a distinctly non-addictive tipple. If one has to drink it with any frequency it comes to taste like Parrish's Chemical Food. Do you remember Parrish's Chemical Food? I don't know what was in it.
Anne	*(amused)* Yes. I do. And there was a green one called Neurophosphates.
Mervyn	Where are the medicaments of yester year? And Gregory's Powders. I remember screaming the house down when they tried to get me to take it as that horrid red powder mixed with water. And cascara sagrada.

Anthony	You must have been very keen on the bowels in those days.
Mervyn	Oh, but we were — or at least our parents were — weren't they, Anne? It's an interesting sidelight on that period. They had a holy terror of constipation. Nowadays people are much more open — so they don't need laxatives. This is perhaps not a very suitable conversation for brandy and cigars.
Anne	Perhaps not. Of course it was a different world, wasn't it? I feel quite lost nowadays. Then one was . . .
Mervyn	"Assured of certain certainties".
Anne	Exactly. And I don't think it was simply because we were in the army. It wasn't just the army. Everyone had his place and seemed to be happy about it on the whole. Of course there was the Depression — but at least you knew where you were.
Anthony	Even if you were on the dole.
Anne	You can't understand how different life was.
Anthony	I understand. If you wanted anything you rang a bell and somebody came running from half a mile away and up three flights of stairs and said "Yes, Ma'am", and you said. "It's rather draughty. Would you shut the window"? It was a great world. I'd have liked it.
Anne	I think people were happier then, and not just the so-called privileged classes. Don't you think so?
Mervyn	I think they may have been. It's not a question one can answer without some sort of yardstick to measure happiness with.
Anne	At least they were more contented. They weren't so neurotic.
Anthony	I doubt it.
Mervyn	You know about contented oysters? They don't produce pearls.
Anthony	If I was an oyster I'm damed if I'd waste my time making pearls. (a) It must be bloody uncomfortable with all that sand inside your striped combinations and (b) what use is a pearl to an oyster anyway? I'm for happy oysters. Christopher, are you for contented oysters or pearl necklaces?

Christopher	Why?
Anthony	You haven't been following. What's the use of all this animated conversation, as Mervyn calls it, if you don't listen.
Christopher	I've been thinking.
Anthony	That'll be the day.
Christopher	*(standing up)* I've been thinking seriously about this book. It's not going to work. Nothing but harm could come of it. I'm afraid we've asked Mr. Dakyns here on false pretences. It's my fault. I should have realised much earlier that it wouldn't work out. All I can say is that I'm sorry. We're all sorry . . .
Anne	But Christopher, why? What do you mean?
Christopher	I'd rather not say any more.
Mervyn	That will leave us with a rather difficult silence.
Christopher	I'm prepared to discuss it with you alone but not . . .
Anthony	Not in front of the children.
Christopher	If you like.
Anne	I don't like it at all. It wasn't you who invited Mervyn down here. In fact you've shown very little interest in the whole matter. Why should you take it upon yourself now to . . .
Christopher	As the head of the family I must do what I think best . . .
Anthony	Oh, Jesus.
Anne	I really don't see that in a matter of this sort . . .
Anthony	There are other parts of the family's anatomy . . .
Christopher	And you keep your nasty little mouth shut.
Anne	Now, be quiet both of you. I've had about enough. Mervyn, I'm so sorry. This must be dreadfully embarrassing for you.
Mervyn	I . . .
Anne	I've got used to it, more or less; but before a guest it seems to me quite deplorable . . .
Christopher	*(to Anthony)* Go on. Apologise.
Anthony	You make me sick.
Christopher	Do as I say.
Anthony	Go to hell.

Anne	Now, stop it, Anthony.
Anthony	I'm sorry.
Anne	Christopher, give Mervyn some more brandy and let's try to behave ourselves decently and sensibly.
Christopher	I'm just trying to be helpful.
Anne	Not very successfully, I must say.
Christopher	That's a very unfair remark. I've been giving a lot of thought to this business — for weeks. I told you when you got Mervyn's letter that I didn't much like the idea. Can't you see I'm trying to do what's best? It's my duty to give you my opinion. Of course, you never listen to me anyway. You never have. You just expect me to be — I don't know — a pale imitation of father; and the paler the better.
Anne	That's not true. Naturally I've expected you boys to be proud that you had a distinguished father. It was your own decision to go into the army. But when you didn't make a go of it, neither of us raised the slightest objection to your changing your mind.
Christopher	I did make a go of it. It was just that, at the time, there seemed to be less prospects for promotion . . . And I couldn't stand the old man always pulling strings.
Anne	Well, it would have been ridiculous for you not to get into the Regiment.
Anthony	*(to Mervyn)* Here. Let me fill it. *(He fills both their glasses)*
Christopher	It's water under the bridge. Forget it.
Anne	For some reason you always seemed to resent your father.
Christopher	Forget it.
Anne	I won't. I can't forget it. Because that's why you're trying to stop this book from being written.
Christopher	Nonsense.
Anne	Isn't it?
Christopher	No, it is not.
Anne	What is the reason, then?
Christopher	Do as you damn please. *(He goes to fill his glass)*
Anne	I do think some explanation is necessary.

Christopher	I've said enough.
Anthony	Hear. Hear.
Anne	Anthony. What is it all about?
Anthony	It's a game called Happy Families. Christopher is being Master Fool, the General's masterful son. I like that.
Christopher	Ha. Ha.
Mervyn	May I try to say something helpful?
Anne	I don't think it's for you to do the explaining.
Mervyn	I wasn't going to do any explaining, but I want to listen to Christopher's objections. Let me concede that if you really convince me, Christopher, that my book would be harmful in some way . . .
Anne	How could it be harmful?
Mervyn	I'm sure it couldn't, but perhaps Christopher will tell us.
Christopher	I never said that.
Mervyn	Very well. When we met earlier today it seemed to me that you all wanted me to write it. Let's go back to that position. Would you like to say *why* you wanted me to write it? What was it you hoped the book would do? Christopher?
Christopher	I'm not saying any more.
Mervyn	Would you like to do that, Anne?
Anne	I'll try. Everybody's had another brandy but me.

Anthony takes her glass

Thank you, dear. My husband was everything I could have hoped for in a man. In those days it was considered very honourable to be an officer in the army, and I was very proud to be married to an officer. John was a Captain, and to be a Captain at 34 was an achievement then. And although he was as gay and full of fun as they all were, he was also deeply serious. He'd been through the first war, of course, and he'd seen the value of religion. His grandfather had been a minister in the Church of Scotland and although his father went into business — and did very well — he, too, had this great sense of service. He was always involved in what were called "good

works". John inherited from both of them this
extraordinary sense of right and wrong. And if he
knew that something, or some person, even, was
wrong, he would have nothing to do with them. But
he wasn't at all rigid or puritanical — far from it. He
just had high standards — for himself and for other
people. In the army, of course, you weren't expected
to be a saint. We had tremendous parties and
expeditions. It all seems so innocent, now, looking
back. We liked being abroad and he enjoyed being a
Military Attache. It was fun. We always seemed to be
going to formal parties. But he was happiest with his
own Regiment. He loved tradition and he loved
soldiers. He would go and visit the barracks at night —
before he went to bed — even the Detention Barracks
if one of his men was in trouble. None of the others
ever did. They loved him, of course. And he was a
clever man. We had some great talk. I remember there
was a Padre at Colchester who would come round
nearly every evening and argue . . . Jack was very tall;
and dark. You've seen photographs?

Mervyn   I met him.

Anne   Of course you did. How silly of me. They would sit
            till all hours talking about politics. By then, of course,
            we were all beginning to feel the way the world was
            going, and I think it strengthened his resolve to equip
            himself utterly for the job of soldiering. In many ways
            he hated it. He hated war, more than anyone I've
            ever met. But he saw that it had to be done. That
            something wrong — evil — would have to be fought,
            and that it had better be done well. The War found
            him fully prepared. I thought of him as a knight
            riding out to defend what we believed in. I did. The
            boys can mock me. But that's how I felt.

                         A pause

            You know about during the War. France the first
            time and . . . how he remade the battalion. And then
            North Africa and Italy. Alexander told me that John
            was his most brilliant commander in Tripoli. I have
            his letter somewhere. You know he lost less than half
            a dozen men in the whole advance on Tripoli. Then he
            was home for three or four months before D day. He

was training, of course. He never stopped. But we had
a little house and he was in such tremendous spirits.
He knew we were going to win, and he was aching to
get at them. And yet he was very gentle and he used
to take days off and we would go down to the marshes
and spend hours watching the bird life. He knew so
much about it. I think it was the happiest time of my
life — in spite of the War.

Anthony   And I was conceived.

Anne   Hush. Then, even in the terrible fighting round Caen,
his letters were always confident. He became
frightfully tired and I pleaded with him to take some
leave. And he did hand over for a fortnight and went
back to the coast, and it was there that . . .
I never really found out what happened. They said it
was a nervous breakdown, but he never had any
nervous trouble — or mental trouble, anything like
that. He could easily have gone back to his command.
There were jealousies, of course. There always are
when people are successful and popular, and when he
was a guest with his old regiment; he wouldn't have
a nervous breakdown when he was among his friends,
would he? Of course they hushed it up but there was
some dirty work somewhere. They wouldn't even
let me see him. He didn't write for weeks. They
wouldn't tell me where he was. He was shut up in
some mental hospital in the north — in Scotland.
How could they treat him like that? *(She weeps)*

Christopher Mother. Don't cry. That's why I don't think we
should have a book. It upsets you too much.

Anne   I'm sorry. He always hated that kind of thing. He'd
no time for army psychiatrists. At the end of the War
there seemed to be more of them than officers. He
believed in self-discipline and he thought they just
encouraged people to be cowards. He didn't believe
in wallowing in emotions. It must have been terrible
for him. When he came home he was very quiet and
he wouldn't talk about it, even to me. He went for
long walks . . . Of course we assumed he would be
going back to France. Or I did. Then we got this
letter posting him to Aldershot.

Mervyn	That came as a blow to him.
Anne	A terrible, terrible blow. I think in a way he was expecting it. That's what finally . . . destroyed him, that letter. That he couldn't go back to his friends and his soldiers.
Mervyn	I can understand
Anne	He'd always been good at training soldiers, brilliant. But he just seemed to have lost all heart for it, after what they'd done to him.
Mervyn	Who were "they"? Who did he blame for it?
Anne	I never heard him blame anyone. It wasn't his nature.

A pause

Mervyn	And what you hoped for, from the book, was . . .?
Anne	To put it right, I suppose.
Mervyn	I don't quite . . .
Anne	It was unfair. And it meant that . . . well, everything was . . . thrown away. He never got the credit for all the other things . . . in his life.
Mervyn	Yes.
Anne	And I hope you'll find out the truth about the whole sordid business.
Mervyn	You don't accept that he had some sort of . . . nervous breakdown?
Anne	Certainly not.
Mervyn	When he did come home — after he had been in Scotalnd he must have given you some sort of explanation.
Anne	You don't understand. For Jack the army was . . . It was almost a religion. To some extent I was a part of it. I was an army wife. But I wasn't allowed into the inner sanctum. Of course it is a very masculine thing, the army. I'm not one of those women who want to get into every male preserve. I'm old fashioned.
Mervyn	But when he came back from Scotland . . .?
Anne	When he came back he told me he hadn't been well, that he was tired, that he didn't really feel up to going on. He tried to make it convincing. They felt he needed a rest . . . But he let me know that at the

	heart of it, this was one of those special areas. It was the army's business and I wasn't to talk about it. It was difficult, of course, but I always respected his principles.
Christopher	I think it was a very good principle. We'd do much better to stick to it.
Anthony	Bottle it up.
Mervyn	And no one else spoke to you about . . . what had happened?
Anne	I was desperately anxious and they wouldn't let me go up to see him. Then Colonel Johnstone came to see me, who was on his Staff, but I couldn't listen to him. He was a silly man. John never liked him much.
Mervyn	But what did he tell you? Please. What did he say?
Anne	Oh, I've forgotten. It was some nonsense about a parade. I think he said my husband had turned up improperly dressed. I never heard such nonsense. John was always meticulous about such things. He was always perfectly turned out. I had his dress uniform specially sent out. But it was simply an excuse. I didn't listen to him. As if it mattered.
Mervyn	I see.
Anne	Of course it was simply a blind; and what a cheap blind. They might have thought of something less silly. No. Jealousy was at the bottom of it.
Mervyn	Do you have any evidence for that?
Anne	You keep talking about evidence. How could I have evidence? I'm not a detective. I couldn't go around interviewing half the High Command in the middle of a war, could I? No. We agreed to accept it — for the good of the country, if you like — and pretend nothing had happened. But the wound was very deep. It was very deep indeed — for both of us. John carried on with what duties he had until the time came for him to retire. It was difficult when people asked questions. We had to pretend that he'd been ill. But there was nothing the matter until they put him into that horrid hospital. They could have killed him.
	After a long pause

Mervyn	I think we both want the same thing. On the whole. Certainly, General Black-Matheson has not received the credit, the attention, that his achievements deserved. I would like to write about both his achievements and his personality. His achievements were considerable, but there was something very impressive and engaging about his character and his personality. This is mainly what I want to write about. On the other hand I'm afraid that the biographer in me cannot but be struck by the drama of the ending of his career. I mean the ending to all intents and purposes, when he lost his command.
Anne	I can understand that.
Mervyn	I don't think it's dishonourable to be interested in that. We are all interested in life . . . and fate . . . and its peculiar quirks. *Nihil humani alienum.* But I should also confess that I can't agree with you that there was any kind of conspiracy.
Anne	But why else should they send him home?
Mervyn	That becomes rather the question. I believe that he did have some kind of nervous breakdown. Suppose that, under this very considerable strain, he had had . . . some kind of amnesia? I wouldn't have thought anyone could regard that as shameful. Everybody has a breaking point.
Anne	John did not have a nervous breakdown. There was nothing like that in either of our families. I'm not prepared to talk about it if you're going to go on saying that.

A pause

Mervyn	You don't want me to undertake this book?
Anne	Yes. Christopher, what am I to say?
Christopher	I've told you already. I can't see any good coming from it.
Anne	I do so want to do the right thing. What do you mean by a nervous breakdown? Do you mean he was temporarily mad? That he had a brainstorm?
Mervyn	These are very old-fashioned terms.
Anne	I don't understand the modern ones.

Mervyn	I don't think he was mad. No.
Anne	Then why did they put him in an asylum?
Christopher	It wasn't an asylum.
Anne	It was a hospital for mental patients.
Christopher	It wasn't an asylum.
Mervyn	Almost everyone I know has been . . . at least to *see* a psychiatrist. People go in and out of that kind of hospital, or clinic, nowadays, as often as they go on holiday.
Anne	Well, I don't know anybody like that.
Mervyn	We know he had been under a very considerable strain.
Anne	You mean he cracked up? That's what they all said, and it's not true. I know it's not true.
Mervyn	I didn't say that..
Anne	I think it's hopeless. We totally disagree. Oh, well. It's funny, when you wrote to me I had the oddest sensation. You know how sometimes a letter seems to say something to you quite different from what is actually written down? I got the strangest feeling that you were somebody who really might understand. Please don't feel I don't appreciate what you've done. It was very good of you to come down here and talk to us. I'm afraid you'll feel you've wasted your time. I'm sorry. I did so hope we could have a nice, good book, about my husband. But Christopher's right, isn't he? It wouldn't work. You were never happy about it?
Christopher	No, never.
Mervyn	And Anthony? You've been very silent.
Anthony	You know, it's terrible. It really is.
Anne	What is? What do you mean?
Anthony	Here are four adult human beings. We've been talking for half an hour about something that happened twenty-five years ago. And we've all been pretending that we don't know what it was. Why? Mother, you know what happened. I know you know, although you've never talked about it. I know you were told. Christopher knows. Even Mervyn knows. He does.

	Mervyn knew before any of you. He was almost there. Why are we pretending we don't know?

Mervyn knew before any of you. He was almost
there. Why are we pretending we don't know?

Anne   I think you've had too much brandy. Be quiet.

Anthony   Oh, and stop giving me orders. You can't keep me
              quiet any longer. What are we all afraid of? Mother,
              we've been keeping quiet about this for twenty-five
              years. Why? It's not worth it. We know what
              happened, but it wasn't anything terrible. You're
              bloody miserable because your husband took his
              clothes off one Sunday morning twenty-five years
              ago.

Anne   What a ridiculous thing to say.

Anthony   That's it. That's why. Otherwise you'd be a contented,
              fulfilled, General's widow with your head held high
              and a lifetime of beautiful memories. But for that; but
              for that tiny incident it would all have added up. You
              need never have questioned a moment of it.

Anne   I don't question it. I don't question anything about
              my life. I'm very proud of my husband's life.

Anthony   Oh, no you're not. You're trying to stop Mervyn
              writing about it.

Anne   That's quite ridiculous.

Anthony   You told Mervyn you'd wanted a nice book and by
              that you meant that you wanted him to tell a pack of
              lies about plots and conspiracies in the High
              Command.

Anne   I wanted him to find out the truth.

Anthony   You *know* the truth. Father appeared in the nude to
              take a ceremonial parade.

Anne   It's not true. It isn't true.

Christopher   Tony. Cut it out.

Anthony   He didn't get on to the parade ground. Everything
              was hushed up. But it happened. Didn't it?

Anne   That was one of the lies they spread about . . .

Anthony   Mervyn? True or false?

                        A pause

Mervyn   I think that's what happened.

Christopher   I don't think there's any use in . . .

Anthony   Christopher?

Christopher	We'll never know exactly what happened. It . . .
Anthony	True or false? What do you think?
Christopher	You're being melodramatic.
Anthony	Mother. What I've said is true. Isn't it?
Anne	I'm not prepared to be cross-questioned by you.
Anthony	Mother. Is is true or false? You know it's true.
Anne	Leave me alone. I'm ashamed of you.
Anthony	Kit. It's true. You know it's true. Sergeant Major Macdonald told me and he was *there*. Say it's true.
Christopher	Something like that happened. Now shut up about it.
Anne	Kit. How could you? I don't know what you're trying to prove. You've no respect for anyone — even your father. You're both against me and you don't give a damn for your father's reputation. You're only concerned with yourselves. Well, I'm going to have nothing to do with it. I know it's very fashionable nowadays to make up all sorts of nasty stories about famous people, but I'll have no part of it.
Anthony	Let me say one more thing. Let's be very calm. Look. Here's my argument. I have an argument.
Christopher	Cut it out.
Anthony	No. Listen. Mother. We all know it's true. What I say is true. Father, for whatever reason, and under whatever kind of strain, took all his clothes off and was going out on parade. No. Please. That's my first proposition. Second proposition. In the particular context of the regiment and army, and all sorts of other droll goings on at the time, it was necessary to send him back to England. Not acceptable behaviour; but he had lots of good and reasonable excuses. He'd had a hard war. He was tired. He was probably drunk. No matter. It wasn't an acceptable piece of behaviour, so they put his trousers on and sent him home.
Christopher	You don't need to be vulgar.
Anthony	We all, in our heart of hearts, don't we, Mother, know that that's what happened? Well, if it happened the army behaved perfectly reasonably, according to its lights, according to most people's lights, in giving him the chop. That sort of thing just wasn't on. Can't have

	that sort of thing in the army. But why do *we* have to accept their judgement?
Anne	Do we accept their judgement? Have we accepted their judgement?
Anthony	Of course we have — you more than anyone.
Anne	I have?
Anthony	You've accepted that this was a terrible thing; that we mustn't talk about it; that it was something dreadful.
Anne	I . . .
Anthony	Why not? Why not, for God's sake? A man takes his clothes off. Is that the end of the world?
Mervyn	I think it's a little more complicated than that, if I may say so.
Anthony	I *don't* think it's more complicated than that. That's my whole point.
Anne	But why?
Anthony	Because he was sickened by the whole thing. Because he'd seen people dressed up as Germans shooting people dressed up as Frenchmen. He'd seen people dressed up as soldiers shoot mothers and children and babes in arms. And this band — a full military band in the middle of the War — playing jolly marching tunes to tell them all it was a great, splendid, glorious march to victory. Rule Britannia. And several hundred living, breathing, human beings with wives and children and sweethearts and little shops and jobs in garages, and gardens, and climbing boots . . . the lot of them lined up like ninepins, toy soldiers, polished up till you could smell the soap, out there on the square. For what? For what — honest to God — for Black Jack Matheson to trot out and walk up and down saying, "Jolly good show", and then nip back into the Mess for a couple of gins and tonic. This in the middle of a war; when they were killing people, hundreds of them, thousands. Can you see him wrestling into his stiff collar, half strangling himself with the stud? Squeezing into those ridiculous boots; smothering himself in gold braid and medals?
Anne	He loved dressing up. You don't understand.

Anthony	Perhaps I don't understand. But at least *I'm* trying to.
Anne	He was quite different from you.
Christopher	He wouldn't feel like that.
Anthony	All right. Then he didn't. But whatever he felt like, he chucked the lot of it off and trotted down the stairs as naked as an angel.
Anne	No. He couldn't have.
Anthony	He did. Mother, let's never mind the reasons. Forget about why. But admit that it happened. He did it. You know he did it. Please. I won't go on about it, but please, for your own sake, admit. Admit it happened. We all know it happened. Say you know it happened. Just say it.

Anne finally nods her head

	Thank you. That's something. That's a big step forward.
Christopher	I can't see what you've gained by it, I must say.
Anthony	A minute; a minute.
Anne	I don't want to talk any more about it. Mr. Dakyns, what must you think of us?
Mervyn	I think I agree with Anthony; that there's virtue in getting at the truth. Perhaps the truth isn't so terrible after all.
Anne	I feel so ashamed.
Anthony	Why ashamed? There's nothing to be ashamed about.
Christopher	Leave it. You've said enough
Anthony	No, I haven't. Why should you feel ashamed?
Anne	It's all very well for you to talk. I've lived under this cloud for twenty-five years.
Anthony	What cloud?
Anne	Really.
Anthony	What cloud? It was nothing. Nothing.
Anne	Nothing? It destroyed your father's career. It destroyed his life.
Anthony	And it destroyed Christopher's life and it did it's best to destroy mine. And for what? For what? It was a nothing and it happened in five minutes twenty-five years ago. Then it was all over. It should have been forgotten.

Anne	Now you're being tiresome and silly.
Anthony	We should have laughed at it.
Anne	I've let you go on talking far too long. Kit is quite right. We shouldn't have stirred the whole thing up. It does no good wallowing in that sort of thing. I'm going to make some more coffee. You'll have some, Mervyn, won't you?
Mervyn	Not for me. Thank you.
Anthony	Will you listen to me?
Anne	We've all listened far too much. Anyway I want some more coffee.
Anthony	Don't go away. Please.
Anne	Now, I've had enough of this. It's fine for you to talk but you don't care about anything. You just slop about. You spoil things. Your generation has no respect and no morals and no standards, so don't you set yourself up to lecture *me* about how to behave.
Anthony	I'm not lecturing you.
Anne	Yes, you are. And stop it.

> *Anthony cannot think of anything to say, torn between fury and depression. A pause*

Anne	I'll make some coffee.
Mervyn	No please. As Anthony would seem to be temporarily deprived of speech perhaps I can venture a comment or two. It seems to me, if I may say so, that Anthony has made a point, and it has taken us a little further on. We have spent some time, and energy, shadow boxing but the cat is now out of the bag. I really feel — and I am fairly optimistic Anne, that you will forgive my saying so — that it would be unsuitable for us to try and put it back again. On the other hand I am with you in agreeing that we don't want to subject this unfortunate pussy to an unpleasant and messy post-mortem examination. But I don't think we have to. Let me put it like this. May we just accept for the purposes of my argument that the army behaved reasonably?
Anne	I won't accept that.
Anthony	The one thing you couldn't accept was that father took his clothes off and danced about in the nude.

Anne	How dare you say that.
Christopher	Shut up.
Anthony	But it's true. That was the only thing. Father was worse than any of us. Because he felt he'd let the regiment down he punished himself by taking a vow of silence about the whole thing.
Christopher	And quite right too. He lost his head and behaved in a damn silly and shameful fashion. We've all suffered for it and quite right. And now let's bloody well forget it.
Anthony	*(furious)* But you haven't forgotten it.
Christopher	Yes we have. What do you want us to do?
Mervyn	Anthony wants you to get it out of your system.
Christopher	Ridiculous.
Anne	I have such a headache.
Anthony	I think we're all mad. I mean this family.
Christopher	The only one who's mad is you. You hang about Chelsea dressed like a bloody male prostitute with flowery ties and shirts and long hair. You look like a woman. I don't know what your job is. You call yourself some kind of artist, but all you seem to do is go to parties and chat up little girls in mini skirts. That's what's wrong with the world. People are too damned self-indulgent. Homosexuals and dope-addicts and perverts write in the newspapers and everyone's expected to follow them and make life one great, splendid orgy of sex and drink and marijuana, and nobody's expected to have any sort of responsibility or discipline. I'm damned if you'll lay down the law to me. Either of you. The old man kept quiet about it, and a bloody good thing, too. Every honourable person did. In those days people had a damn sight better sense of what was proper and what wasn't. You think you've a God-given right to behave like a gutter cat and be as self-indulgent as you please, but not everyone agrees with you. Some people have certain standards, and don't you forget it.
Anthony	I have standards myself.
Christopher	I've seen little sign of it.

Anthony	I believe in being honest for one thing.
Christopher	Do you? Well. I've admitted that father lost his head and . . . behaved ridiculously. He let everyone down. I've admitted that. Haven't I? And now bloody well shut up about it.
Anthony	I won't shut up about it.
Anne	Christopher . . .
Anthony	Can't you see what we're trying to tell you?
Christopher	You've nothing to tell me.
Anthony	Mervyn, you tell them.
Mervyn	I . . .
Christopher	You keep out of this.
Anne	I can't stand any more of this.
Christopher	We've suffered enough because of this damn mess without . . .
Anthony	*(shouting)* It wasn't a mess. Can't you see it wasn't a disaster. He didn't lose the War. Nobody got killed. Nobody got hurt. He just took his fucking clothes off, you nit.
Christopher	Don't you shout at me. Mother, I think we must stop this conversation. If you'd listened to me. We should have stopped this whole thing. Mr. Dakyns, I hold you responsible for this. I suppose it's very liberal, as you'd call it, to stir up this kind of thing.
Mervyn	I would call myself a liberal, yes . . .
Christopher	But you have to draw a line somewhere and, in my view it would be much better if people exercised some self-control and left other people alone.
	Anthony has been furiously throwing off his clothes and presents himself, naked, to Anne
Anthony	Look, mother. This is all it was. I've no clothes on. Look at me. Look at me.
	Anne covers her eyes
	I'm your son. You made me like this.
Anne	I must go. I can't bear this.
	She makes for the door but Anthony rushes to cut her off

Anthony	Don't go away. Stop mother. *(He bars the door)* What are you afraid of? It's only me.
Christopher	Tony. Get out of the way. Get away from that door.
Anthony	Why? What are you afraid of?
Christopher	*(shouting)* Get away from the door.
Anne	I can't stand it.

> *She half faints and half wrestles with Anthony. Christopher seizes a bottle from the table and fells Anthony with a blow on the head. He falls to the ground*

Anne	Kit. What have you done? Anthony. Are you all right?
Christopher	Tony. Are you all right? The stupid fool.

> *They carry him to the sofa where Anne tends the wound on his head. Mervyn brings a rug.*

Anne	My sweetheart: are you all right? Christopher, really.

> *Christopher goes out*

Anthony	Yes. I'm all right. You nearly killed me. Oh, my head. *(he sits up)* Ouch. What? What was I supposed to have done? The terrible Black-Matheson sin of taking my clothes off.

> *He collapses again on Anne who embraces him. She is in tears*

Anne	Sweetheart. Sweetheart.

> *Mervyn picks up the rug from in front of the fire and places it discreetly over Anthony*
>
> *Curtain*

ACT TWO

SCENE TWO

The same. It is twenty minutes later. Mervyn solus. He is helping himself to some brandy and is a little nervous. He looks at himself in a mirror and adjusts his hair and his tie as if to satisfy himself that everything is in place, that he is the assured, sophisticated, competent, intellectual he knows himself to be. He picks up a magazine and sits, with what air of relaxed assurance he can muster, on the sofa.

Anthony comes in

Anthony	*(looking at Mervyn's glass)* Quite right. I'll have one too. And thank you.
Mervyn	For what?
Anthony	For being on my side.
Mervyn	I was on my own side.
Anthony	Were you?
Mervyn	Cheers.
Anthony	*(sitting down)* Cheers. At least you weren't on their side.
Mervyn	I thought it was a brave gesture — *un beau geste.*
Anthony	I don't know. Was it? It wouldn't do any good.
Mervyn	It may have done.
Anthony	I doubt it. People don't like being upset.
Mervyn	I don't like being upset myself, but sometimes it's good for you.
Anthony	Did I upset you?
Mervyn	Gracious, no. I was speaking in general principles.
Anthony	I don't think anything's good for people. They just go on being. The idea that we can get better is based on . . . I don't know.
Mervyn	I am on your side.
Anthony	Oh, don't try to seduce me, now. That would be too much for one night.
Mervyn	Nothing was further from my mind. Damn it, you've broken my train of thought. No, I want to discuss this sensibly.
Anthony	Discuss what? I don't want to discuss anything.
Mervyn	I'm sure you were right — trying to force them to understand. You made a very good case.
Anthony	But I spoilt it by going too far.
Mervyn	I wouldn't say that.
Anthony	You liked my little strip-tease act?
Mervyn	I thought it was charming.
Anthony	I was always a bit of an exhibitionist.

Mervyn	*(getting up)* No. Be serious. You were trying to make a perfectly valid point. In the first place . . .
Anthony	No. Don't let's be serious. I'm tired.
Mervyn	You mustn't be tired. This is the time to gallop down the hill, to throw in the cavalry, take them on the flank.
Anthony	I don't want to. I've exposed enough flanks for one campaign. At least I don't want to enough. If they want it their way, let them have it.
Mervyn	No. We must pursue them. I think you're within an ace of victory.
Anthony	What victory?
Mervyn	What victory?
Anthony	What victory?
Mervyn	What have you been fighting for?
Anthony	Have I been fighting? Somebody hit me on the head. But I wasn't fighting.
Mervyn	You were fighting for the truth. They've hidden it away and built a great, crawling, dung heap of anxieties and suppressions over it. I was trying to pick away at it in my elderly, academic way; but you showed them the truth in one beautiful gesture.
Anthony	You *are* trying to seduce me.
Mervyn	Now you're being unfair. Be serious. I see far too many young people in College to get excited by a naked body — of either sex.
Anthony	You're getting old.
Mervyn	Yes I am. Thank God.
Anthony	Are you a homosexual?
Mervyn	Certainly not, and I didn't come down here to talk about my sex life.
Anthony	I only asked. It's nice to know these things.
Mervyn	When you're as old as I am, my dear boy, you will realise that you can live a very happy and useful life without being continually obsessed with sex.
Anthony	I'll take you word for it. And you don't get a thrill out of the idea of the old man suddenly appearing in the buff?

Mervyn	Most certainly not. So that's what you were thinking? No. No. When I said before dinner that something had fixed in my mind . . .
Anthony	I didn't think anything. I want to go to sleep.
Mervyn	You mustn't go to sleep. No, I certainly didn't mean anything like that.
Anthony	You did, you know.
Mervyn	No. Absolutely not. And I was shocked — a little shocked, by your strip-tease act, as you call it. Well, I wasn't shocked but it just seemed a little silly and pointless.
Anthony	Oh, you bastard.
Mervyn	I've no doubt you meant it as a significant gesture but what I'm trying to say is that we must pursue this matter on a proper level and develop our argument in a a serious way. When I wrote to your mother . . . Where is she by the way?
Anthony	She's doing the washing up. It's very therapeutic. Then she'll make herself a nice cup of tea and it'll all be as if nothing had happened.
Mervyn	Oh, we can't have that. This is too important.

Listen, Anthony. Your theory is that the General had a sudden mind-blowing vision of the truth, saw the army, the war, regimental parades, the whole elaborate panoply of it, as absurd and in one peremptory gesture declared himself simply a human being — a poor, bare, forked animal. And said, "To hell with it all". So they fixed him. They sent him off to a cold, Scottish loony bin. Is that your view? Are you asleep? Or are you pretending to be asleep? Yes, I thought so.

There is a certain charm in your version, but it doesn't ring true. No. He had a nervous breakdown; and he never really recovered from it. Did he?

He was a very disciplined man; very rigid and self-controlled. And when you sit tightly on the lid it blows up. I keep remembering that odd episode when he stopped shooting — I mean birds and small game. A very odd decision for one who had absorbed the whole military ethic. But was it a rational decision? Or was it the first sign of a deep tension that, later, was going to crack the rock?

Anthony, wake up. You're missing a very brilliant
diagnosis.

Anthony   What's the time?

Mervyn   It's irrelevant. You haven't been listening to what
I'm saying.

Anthony   Yes I have. Tensions.

Mervyn   Yes, there's this tension; between an essentially
humane, even pacific, painter and ornithologist
and his professional career. A soldier, however much
you cover him up in scarlet and ceremony, is paid
to kill his country's enemies. And it was when the
war was nearly over, his violent job nearly ended,
victory in sight; it was *then* that the pressure became
intolerable. You've no idea how interesting a point
of reference it makes for my book. And the tragedy
is that we have such a very tentative hold on the
cooling surface of our very minor planet that we *do
have* to organise ourselves in that sort of rigid and
disciplined way if we're to survive at all. Certainly
in a war: certainly in the army. Don't you agree? And
yet there is still a tiny, furry, joyful, optimistic little
corner of my soul, if you'll forgive that dreary old
concept, that wants to throw its clothes off and join
in the rout.

Anthony   You say that in your book.

Mervyn   Say what?

Anthony   That the old man was on to something but that you're
too mean-minded to support him.

Mervyn   What?

Anthony   And that the sooner we get rid of these rigid and soul-
destroying social structures, the better.

Mervyn   But I don't think that. I wish I did. But I don't. You
won't even think that yourself in another three
or four years. You'll get married, and settle down,
and worry about schools and income tax. You'll
join the Tory party.

Anthony   I'm beginning to dislike you, Mervyn.

Mervyn   Well, perhaps not the Tory party. But your ideas will
change, I promise you. You haven't read either of my
books?

Anthony	I looked at them on a bookstall.
Mervyn	Well, even the blurbs would show you I'm on your side. You see, even if you're right, your father didn't survive his gesture, his apostasy. It's only the rarest individuals who stick to their guns — or stick to their not having guns — and get away with it. You can't reject the great dogmas of your society. But don't worry. My book will be on your side — on the side of the revolution. It'll be extremely lively and interesting. It'll make you laugh.
Anthony	It'll make me vomit.
Mervyn	I'm going to use the army as representing the last remaining example of a whole middle-class ethic in which self-discipline was the key to comfort and good living. If you become a doctor or an engineer, nowadays, you may have to wash the dishes and put the children to bed. If you become an officer you have servants. Incredible though it seems, the youngest subaltern, fresh from Grammar School by way of Sandhurst, has a servant — to polish his boots, press his little evening trousers and bring him his drinks. He dines at a mahogany table and drinks claret out of silver goblets to the sound of light airs from the regimental band. I promise you, you'll like it. It'll be right up your street.
Anthony	But why do you want to do all this?
Mervyn	It's interesting. It's of the greatest interest. An archaic way of life persisting into a totally changed world; and your father's one amazing gesture trapped in it, like a fly in amber.
Anthony	And that's why you want to write the book?
Mervyn	More or less.
Anthony	But what do you feel about it? Where do you stand?
Mervyn	I'm just a reporter. I observe. I am a camera.
Anthony	You're a white liberal.
Mervyn	You make it sound a fearful term of abuse. But, yes. I'm a liberal; and I'm an off-pink Caucasian.
Anthony	And you're a bloody intellectual.
Mervyn	I own the soft impeachment.
Anthony	But you don't have to behave like one *all* the time.

Mervyn	How else would you know I was a don?
Anthony	I would know you were a don if I saw you stretched out on a mortuary slab.
Mervyn	Would you?
Anthony	You look like a bloody don. Dead or alive, it makes little difference.

Enter Anne and Christopher

Anne	You said you didn't want any more coffee? You won't change your mind?
Mervyn	No, thank you.
Anne	Poor Mr. Dakyns . . . What an evening you've had. I feel it's so inhospitable to . . . empty the washing machine in front of strangers like that.
Mervyn	I don't feel a stranger.
Anne	It's all been funny, really, hasn't it? A great joke. We haven't quite got used to having a member of the new generation in the house. It's extraordinary how they behave. I think it's terribly funny. And they take themselves so seriously.
Mervyn	Perhaps.
Anne	Every generation's the same. They all want to teach their grandmothers to suck eggs. When I was young I felt just the same. I was a show-off. When I think of the things we used to get up to . . . We wanted to be noticed. We felt that our ideas were terribly important.
Anthony	You think that's what I've been doing this evening? Showing off?
Anne	In a way, yes. But I understand.
Anthony	Do you honestly think so? Do you understand what I've been trying to tell you? Do you? I've been trying to say that I loved my husband dearly. I didn't know him as a great, gallant, General; he didn't rush about playing wild games with me, as he did with Kit. But I loved him and I loved the thing he did — whatever he meant by it. It was a beautiful thing to do, I think. And if only I'd been able to tell him so — if only I'd known — he might have been happier himself. But instead we've all made ourselves miserable about it for twenty-five years — more. It's we who are insane.
Anne	Now you're being silly. Christopher . . .

Christopher   Mervyn, I'm not much of a reader, so I suppose my opinion doesn't count for much. I haven't read a lot of biographies. Well I read a book about Gladstone. I suppose nowadays you put a lot of things in that. . . well, people don't normally talk about.

Mervyn   That is rather the fashion. Of course people talk about a lot of things they didn't talk about a few years ago.

Christopher   I see. I'm a bit of a dinosaur, as Anthony said. I was brought up with certain standards and I accepted them. I honoured the king, gave my seat to ladies in the bus and put my hand in front of my mouth when I coughed . . . that sort of thing. I believed in God and Winston Churchill and the Empire, even. I used to read the Boy's Own Paper, sleep with the windows open. I have this nicely polished set of standards of behaviour and they're about as useful as the old pennies and threepenny bits, it seems to me. I don't see that the new standards — if you can call them that — are any better and I doubt if I could change if I wanted to. I'm a period piece. I'm just old enough to be out of fashion but not old enough to be an antique. So why should you listen to me? The only thing I can say is that Dad was the same kind of chap. I know he wouldn't have approved of anyone writing the kind of stuff it seems to me you want to write. I'm not criticising you. That kind of thing's probably very popular, and maybe it has something to be said for it. But it seems to me to be just not on as far as father is concerned. Don't you think so?

Anne   Yes. Yes, I think so.

Mervyn   Is that your final word Anne?

Anne   I think so. I really have tried to understand your point of view. And I won't deny that perhaps we haven't been very clever in the way, as a family , we've dealt with . . . The whole thing was such a blow to us. It was so unexpected, so unlike Jack. I still can't believe it happened. He was always so reserved, so polite. When I was a girl we got such excitement out of just a look or a handshake, a little pressure on the arm. I've never forgotten the way a young officer took my hand at a dance, my first dance

when I was only about seventeen. I really believe
that's why I married a soldier. And everybody was so
nice. You could rely on people. Nobody dreamt of
breaking the rules — at least nobody *we* met. It was
too sheltered a life probably. My father was a man of
the very highest moral character. I never met anyone
who matched up to him. Never. He was a really fine
man, in every way. Jack, my husband, was a fine man,
too. We had a lovely wedding, in the garden, in a tent,
the reception. The wedding was beautiful, all our
friends looking their smartest. And Jack in uniform.
His boots looked as if they were made of silver. I
was quite dazzled by them. And that high necked
tunic. And he wore a sword. It was a dream. When he
took his clothes off he was really rather ugly and
bony. And I'd never seen a man . . . like that . . .
before. I was so unhappy. I cried right through our
honeymoon. I pretended it was being away from
home. How silly you must think me. Doesn't it
sound prehistoric? And at first he wouldn't wear
pyjamas. He didn't have a nice skin. He had a terrible
lot of hair. I used to suffocate . . . I loved Jack very
much. He was so kind. So I got over it. We had a
very happy married life. It was just the shock at
first and . . . You undress so easily, Anthony. You
could never understand how difficult it was for my
generation. I'd hardly even seen *myself* without my
clothes on. But it's all changed now and I'm sure
it's for the better. The world's quite different. You
dash about in aeroplanes; and it used to be such an
anxiety to go a hundred miles. But I think it must
have hurt him. At the time. Right away, I think he
must have known. I don't suppose he was very much
more experienced than I was. And he *was* very proud.
Poor Jack. He must have known that I was . . .
repelled by him, just for a moment. Anyway that's
what I think. And then when he was very tired,
exhausted, at the end of his tether . . . I'll tell you
why I don't think you should write a book, Mervyn,
at least not about Jack. It was a private matter — a
private communication — to me. It meant that all
this business of being a General, of commanding
armies, of winning a war . . . that it was all just a way

	of convincing yourself that you were doing something useful.
Mervyn	It was pretext.
Anne	What was that? Yes, I suppose so. I think he wanted to say — what he couldn't put into words — that I should have loved the bony man inside. There you are. I did, of course. Later. What's sad is that it's always too late to make amends. But what you would write about would be all the bits that didn't matter. Don't you think? And it is true that we have spoiled our lives? Surely not?
Christopher	No, no.
Anne	You think we have, Anthony?
Anthony	Why didn't you talk like this years ago?
Anne	It's not easy to talk to one's children, once you get out of the habit. But you do understand? You see why I don't think anybody could write about Jack? You could write a Life of the General, but you couldn't write about the man?
Mervyn	I'd like to write about the man and the General. it is, if I may say so, a story which brings together an extraordinary number of public and private issues. That's what attracts me about it.
Anne	We weren't very public people.
Mervyn	Your husband played an important public role, you mustn't forget.
Christopher	If you would confine yourself to the public aspects . . .
Mervyn	I'm sorry I am not to be confined.
Anne	But surely we've all agreed that there shouldn't be a book?
Christopher	I thought so.
Anne	Anthony?
Anthony	I agree with mother. The only thing that matters about my father's life is something very personal and human and tender; and Mervyn Dakyns guddling about in his entrails in a clumsy fashion isn't going to find it. Anyway he'll write a book that will be full of brilliant social observations and dotted with donnish jokes.
Anne	No. That's unkind, and rather rude.

Mervyn	I don't think so. It seems to me a fairly generous and reasonably accurate assessment of my poor talents as a writer. You use words like tender and human. Nobody who's read any history would say the human race are gentle and tender — though there are some exceptions. Thank God. If he exists. Lady Black-Matheson, Anne, there is an old saying that you should remove your foot from the door step of your neighbour before he wearies of it. I am conscious of having come into your hospitable home as a disruptive force. I'm sorry. It *is* rather late at night, and I think you all probably want to go to bed. I'm most grateful to you for a delightful dinner; and for a most interesting conversation.
Anne	And what is your conclusion?
Mervyn	Conclusion? Oh, about the book. Would you allow me to write to you about it? I realise I shall have to get back to College in the morning. I think there's a train to Town about ten o' clock.
Anne	Oh? Must you? I hoped you would stay for . . . We normally have breakfast about . . . Would you like an egg?
Mervyn	Yes, please. And coffee, if it isn't a bore.
Anne	We always have coffee. I put a hot water bottle in your bed, but if you don't want it please throw it out. It's quite mild but I always think a strange bed feels cold.
Mervyn	Thank you.
Anthony	And you're going to write the book, whatever we think?
Mervyn	*(after a long pause)* I want to go back to my rooms in College and think about it. Nearly everything you've said confirms my feeling that I could write an interesting Life of the General — and one you would all be happy about. But I've quite a lot of things on my plate. It's a matter of how I'm to deploy my time. May I write to you?
Anne	Of course.
Mervyn	Thank you. Well good night.
Anne	Good night. You know your way?

Mervyn	Perfectly.
	He goes out
Anne	He's going to write the book, isn't he? After all those things I've said.
Anthony	It doesn't matter. It'll be a pack of lies, because he's a don, and because . . . Nobody could write it. Not the bit that matters. Perhaps you could dance it.
	Anne begins to put out the lights
Christopher	Why are you putting out the lights?
Anne	Aren't you going to bed?
Christopher	I'm going to have some brandy;
Anne	Well, we can't just leave you sitting alone in the dark.
	They all sit down, Christopher almost takes Anne's hand
Christopher	Yes. Well.
	Curtain
	THE END OF THE PLAY